I0035961

DON'T BE THE MARK; KNOW YOUR ALLEGED INVESTMENT OPPORTUNITIES

DON'T BE THE MARK; KNOW YOUR ALLEGED INVESTMENT OPPORTUNITIES

R Tamara de Silva & Cheryl Fitzpatrick

DON'T BE THE MARK; KNOW YOUR ALLEGED INVESTMENT
OPPORTUNITIES@ 2023 by R Tamara de Silva and Cheryl Fitzpatrick. All
rights reserved.

All rights reserved. No part of this book may be reproduced in any form or by any
electronic means including information storage and retrieval systems, without
written permission in writing from the authors. The only exception is by a
reviewer, who may quote short experts in a review.

Cover designed by R Tamara de Silva

This book is a work of non-fiction but is not intended to be legal advice.

R Tamara de Silva & Cheryl Fitzpatrick
Visit my website at www.desilvalawoffices.com

Printed in the United States of America

First Printing March 2023
Amazon KDP

ISBN: 979-8-218-16841-4

Dedicated to *Star and Jackson*

Table of Contents

Introduction

We are tired of seeing people lose their hard-earned money to get rich opportunities and fraudsters. There will always be get rich schemes and good people defrauded by smooth talking salesmen riding the wave of the next big idea or financial mania. We have seen people give their retirement accounts and hard-earned savings to unregistered con men whether it was for internet companies in the 2000s to crypto schemes and ICOs over the past four years.

We have seen many people taken in by smooth-talking, well-dressed salespeople offering irresistible business opportunities. We have often thought and discussed among ourselves- if only people knew where to go to research these salespeople. If only people knew what questions to ask, and what if any recourse they will have if they hand over money to a friendly stranger. So we decided to do something about it.

Using our experience gained over the course of a combined 48 years of practicing securities and derivatives law, along with a deep bench of knowledge of registration and compliance in the financial markets and white collar criminal defense, we hope you can come to a more informed decision when presented with a business opportunity or get rich scheme.

This book is in not intended to be taken as legal advice. It is not a substitute for seeking legal counsel before investing in anything. It is for people who may not have a securities lawyer or law firm on speed dial, and realistically speaking, that is most people.

Our goal is to empower you with some tools to begin to ask the right questions with which to understand an alleged investment opportunity. This is merely a starting point and guide written in our earnest hope that you avoid being the victim of a financial fraud.

R Tamara de Silva, Esq. & Cheryl Fitzpatrick, Esq.

March 5, 2023
Chicago, Illinois

Chapter One
There are common signs of financial fraud.

1. High-pressure sales tactics: Fraudsters may try to pressure you into making a quick decision or may offer you an investment opportunity that s only available for a limited time. Be wary of

anyone who is pushing you to make a decision before you have had time to research or think it through.

2. Guaranteed returns: No investment can guarantee a return, and anyone who claims otherwise is likely trying to scam you. Be skeptical of any investment opportunity that promises guaranteed returns.

3. Unregistered investments: Make sure that any investment opportunity you are considering is registered with the appropriate regulatory authorities. Unregistered investments are often a red flag for fraud.

4. Lack of documentation: Be wary of any investment opportunity that doesn't provide clear and detailed documentation about the investment, including the risks involved and the fees you will be charged.

5. Unsolicited offers: If you receive an unsolicited offer for an investment opportunity, be especially cautious. Fraudsters

often use cold-calling or email spamming to reach potential victims.

6. Overly complex investments: Some fraudsters may try to confuse you with complex investment opportunities using lots of jargon and acronyms that are difficult to understand. If someone cannot explain the investment in simple terms, it's probably best to avoid it.

7. Missing or inconsistent information: Be on the lookout for any missing or inconsistent information in the investment opportunity. Fraudsters may try to hide important details or provide conflicting information to confuse you.

If you encounter any of these signs, it's best to be cautious and do your due diligence before investing any money. It's always a good idea to consult with a trusted financial advisor or do your own research to make sure you fully understand the risks and potential returns of any investment opportunity.

But there are other signs. Many con people are impeccably dressed and appear to be the manifestation of money and financial success. This is sometimes to hide the fact that they need your money to maintain their very appearance of success.

While it is important to remember that con people come in all shapes and sizes, some use their appearance and lifestyle to gain confidence on the part of their victims that they are real thing.

Elizabeth Holmes: Holmes was the founder of the now-defunct blood-testing company, Theranos. She was known for her glamorous appearance and confident demeanor, which helped her attract high-profile investors and secure a valuation of $9 billion for her company. However, it was later revealed that the technology behind Theranos was fraudulent, and the company was shut down.

Carlos Ghosn: Ghosn was the former CEO of Nissan, and was known for his lavish lifestyle and high-profile position in the automotive industry. However, he was arrested in 2018 on charges of financial misconduct, including underreporting his income and misusing company funds.

Billy McFarland: McFarland was the founder of the ill-fated Fyre Festival, which was billed as a luxurious music festival on a private island but turned out to be a disaster. McFarland was known for his flashy lifestyle and ability to charm investors, but he was later convicted of fraud and sentenced to six years in prison.

Kenneth Lay: Lay was the founder and CEO of Enron, a company that was once one of the largest energy companies in the world. He was known for his high-profile lifestyle, including owning multiple homes and traveling in private jets. However, it was later revealed that Enron had engaged in widespread accounting fraud, and Lay was charged with multiple counts of fraud and conspiracy.

Charles Ponzi: Ponzi was the namesake of the Ponzi scheme, which he used to defraud investors out of millions of dollars in the early 20th century. He was known for his extravagant lifestyle and flamboyant personality, which he used to persuade investors to trust him with their money.

Allen Stanford: Stanford was a financier who once owned a cricket team and a private island. He was known for his lavish lifestyle and was often photographed with high-profile celebrities and politicians. However, it was later revealed that he had run a Ponzi scheme that defrauded investors out of billions of dollars.

So just because someone shows up driving a Lamborghini and wearing a Patek Phillippe does not mean they are necessarily what they are trying to appear to be.

Part of appearance is the gift of charisma and charm. Here again, just because someone is charming and well known, or even widely well regarded, does not mean you should put any less time into researching a potential investment with them.

Bernie Madoff: Madoff ran a Ponzi scheme that defrauded investors out of billions of dollars. He was known for his charismatic personality and ability to persuade investors to trust him with their money.

Jordan Belfort: Belfort was a stockbroker who ran a pump-and-dump scheme, where he artificially inflated the price of stocks and then sold them off for a profit. He was known for his lavish lifestyle and charismatic personality, which he used to persuade investors to buy into his schemes.

Frank Abagnale: Abagnale was a con artist who impersonated various professionals, including a doctor and a pilot, in order to defraud people out of money. He was known for his smooth-talking and ability to charm his way out of difficult situations.

Kevin Trudeau: Trudeau was a TV infomercial pitchman who was convicted of fraud for making false claims about his books and products. He was known for his slick sales pitches and his ability to convince people to buy into his scams.

Victor Lustig: Lustig was a con artist who was known for his charm and his ability to sell people on his scams. He is perhaps best known for selling the Eiffel Tower to a scrap metal dealer in Paris, using his charm and persuasion skills to convince the dealer that he was a government official authorized to sell the landmark.

Financial fraud can be committed by anyone, regardless of their appearance, wealth, or social status. It is always important to be vigilant and do your due diligence before investing any money or entering into any financial transaction.

Chapter Two
Tokens

As the world of cryptocurrency continues to grow, it's important for investors to have a strong understanding of the technology behind it. Digital assets are not going away and it is important to understand that how where and how a digital asset is kept can affect its risk of loss and investment risk profile. One key component of the crypto industry and a good starting point are tokens.

Tokens are a type of digital asset that can represent a variety of things, such as a unit of value, or access to a particular service. Tokens are digital assets that are created and managed using blockchain technology. They can represent a variety of things, including a unit of value, access to a particular service, or ownership in a particular asset. Tokens are often associated with the world of cryptocurrency and are used as a means of exchange for goods and services within decentralized networks.

There are two main types of tokens: utility tokens and security tokens. Utility tokens are designed to provide access to a particular service or platform. For example, a utility token could be used to access a particular decentralized application (dApp) or to pay for a particular service within a network. Utility tokens are not considered securities, as their primary purpose is to provide access to a particular product or service.

Security tokens, on the other hand, are tokens that are designed to represent ownership in a particular asset, such as stocks, bonds, or real estate. Security tokens are subject to regulation, as they are considered securities under U.S. law. This means that security tokens must comply with securities laws and regulations, including registration with the Securities and Exchange Commission (SEC) and compliance with disclosure requirements.

Security tokens are subject to greater regulatory scrutiny. This is because they represent ownership in a particular asset and are therefore subject to the same laws and regulations as traditional securities. In contrast, utility tokens are generally not subject to the same level of regulation, as their primary purpose is to provide access to a particular service or platform.

Another difference between utility tokens and security tokens is that security tokens may offer investors certain rights, such as the right to receive dividends or the right to vote on certain matters related to the underlying asset. Utility tokens, on the other hand, typically do not offer investors any ownership rights or other privileges beyond access to the associated service or platform.

In conclusion, tokens are digital assets that can represent a variety of things, from units of value to ownership in particular assets. There are two main types of tokens: utility tokens and security tokens. Utility tokens provide access to a particular service or platform, while security tokens represent ownership in a particular asset and are subject to greater regulatory scrutiny. Understanding the differences between these two types of tokens is important for investors looking to participate in the world of cryptocurrency and blockchain technology.

When considering investing in a token, it's important to understand the basics of what a token is and how it works. Tokens can be registered with various regulatory bodies, depending on the jurisdiction and the type of token. For example, some tokens may be registered with the Securities and Exchange Commission (SEC) in the

United States, while others may be registered with different regulatory bodies in other countries.

If a token is not registered with any regulatory body, it may be considered an unregistered security. This means that it may be subject to additional risks and may not have the same legal protections as registered securities.

It's also important to understand where a token will reside. Some tokens may be held on a centralized exchange, which is a platform that acts as a middleman between buyers and sellers.

Tokens held on a centralized exchange or entity can present several potential problems for investors. Some of these problems include:

Lack of transparency: Centralized exchanges are owned and operated by a single entity, which means that they have control over the trading and custody of assets. This can create a lack of transparency, as investors may not be able to see how their assets are being handled or where they are being stored.

Risk of hacking: Centralized exchanges are a prime target for hackers, as they hold large amounts of cryptocurrency and other digital assets. In the event of a hack, investors may lose their assets and have no recourse for recovery.

Protection against commingling of assets: Centralized exchanges may commingle assets, which means that investors' assets may be mixed with those of other investors. This can create a risk of loss if the exchange experiences financial difficulties or if assets are mismanaged.

Custody: Centralized exchanges are responsible for custody of investors' assets. If an exchange does not have proper security measures in place, investors' assets may be at risk of theft or loss.

Dependence on a single entity: Centralized exchanges are owned and operated by a single entity, which means that investors are dependent on that entity for the trading and custody of their assets. If that entity experiences financial difficulties or is shut down, investors may lose their assets.

To mitigate these risks, investors may choose to use decentralized exchanges or custody solutions, which are not owned or operated by a single entity. Decentralized exchanges use blockchain technology to facilitate peer-to-peer transactions, which eliminates the need for a centralized intermediary. Decentralized custody solutions, such as hardware wallets or self-custody, give investors full control over their assets and eliminate the risk of commingling or loss due to a centralized entity.

In conclusion, while centralized exchanges and custody solutions may offer convenience and ease of use, they can present several potential problems for investors. To mitigate these risks, investors may choose to use decentralized exchanges or custody solutions, which offer greater transparency, security, and control over their assets. Tokens may be held on a blockchain, which is a decentralized ledger that records all transactions in a secure and transparent manner.

In addition to understanding where a token is held, it's also important to understand what it does. Tokens can have a wide range of functions, from providing access to a particular service or platform to serving as a form of currency or investment.

When investing in a token, it's important to read and understand the contract associated with the token. This contract will outline the terms and conditions of the investment, including the rights and responsibilities of the investor and the issuer of the token.

It's also important to note that investing in a token is different from a traditional bank deposit. While bank deposits are insured by the government, investments in tokens are not. This means that investors must be prepared to accept a certain level of risk when investing in tokens. As in the case of FTX or BlockFI, among others, when a centralized exchange takes custody of your tokens and fails, you have no recourse other than to get in line behind creditors in bankruptcy court. This process can take years and you may still not recover the value of your tokens or anything at all.

To invest wisely in the crypto industry, it is crucial to grasp the fundamentals of tokens. Researching the regulatory status, understanding its purpose and where it is held, and carefully reading the associated contract are essential for making informed decisions and mitigating risks.

Chapter Three
Custody, Commingling and Keys

In the world of traditional finance, a custodian is an entity that takes custody of a client's assets and holds and protects assets on the client's behalf. This can include assets such as stocks, bonds, and other financial instruments. The custodian is responsible for ensuring that the assets are safe and secure, and for protecting them against loss, theft, or misuse.

In the futures markets, custodians of customer funds are highly regulated, independently audited, and have historically been one of the safest industries for the protection of customer funds. U.S.

regulated custodians of customer funds in the futures world, segregate customer funds from the funds of the firm, so that in the event the firm or one customer has a financial issue, the customer funds are not affected. Additionally, futures regulations prohibit commodity futures brokerage firms from using the funds of one customer to cover obligations of a separate customer. This further protects customer funds from misuse by the firm.

Because in the futures world, customer funds are never commingled with the custodian firm's funds. Customer funds are protected from contagion if the firm encounters a financial issue. A firm's trading operations are ring-fenced from customer funds. The futures markets do an excellent job in their custodial function, and are regulated by the U.S. Commodities Futures Commission (CFTC) and the National Futures Association (NFA).

In the U.S. securities world, which covers virtually everything other than currencies, futures contracts, options on futures contracts, swaps and derivatives, custodians of customers assets are regulated by the U.S. Securities and Exchange Commission (SEC) and the Financial Industry Regulatory Authority (FINRA).

In the world of crypto, however, the term "custody" is used more loosely. Many "custody" providers offer hot wallets, which are digital wallets that are connected to the internet. Hot wallets are designed to keep funds liquid and accessible, but they also come with greater security risks, as they are more vulnerable to hacking and cyber-attacks.

Furthermore, many custody providers are not actually holding the assets for you; they are simply providing you with a tool to hold the assets yourself. This means that even if you are using a custody provider, you still need to take responsibility for the security and protection of your assets.

The fall of FTX in November of 2022, which went from a valuation in excess of $32 billion to bankruptcy in a matter of weeks, illustrated the weaknesses of centralized cryptocurrency exchanges that take custody of client funds. Though the clients of FTX signed terms of service agreements where they were ensured that their funds would be held safely, what this meant without any actual mechanism to ensure that client funds were segregated and not commingled with firm funds, was little to nothing.

Until the centralized crypto exchanges and custodians mimic the custodial practices of their CFTC and SEC regulated counterparts, an investor has to understand that their only protection is their faith and the word of the custodial firms principals and operators.

Another difference between regulated custodian like exchanges in the futures and securities world, and crypto custodians, is that there are generally no independent audits of the firm's financial condition or any way to know that client funds are continually being kept safely. Because there are no independent audits to ascertain a custodial firm's financial picture and liabilities, just being given a proof of reserves assurance is not enough.

Look for regulated entities such as banks, brokerage firms or trusts that have a fiduciary duty to safeguard their client funds in segregated accounts and protect these same funds from loss, misuse and theft.

Also ask if your assets are insured against loss. In traditional finance, the Federal Deposit Insurance Corp (FDIC) is a government agency that provides insurance for deposits held at member banks in case of a bank failure. The insurance provided by the FDIC is backed by the full faith and credit of the U.S. government. The FDIC offers insurance coverage up to $250,000 per depositor, per FDIC-insured bank.   To find out if your bank is an FDIC member bank, go to https://banks.data.fdic.gov/bankfind-suite/

For digital assets, it is generally safer to self-custody your assets by keeping your keys yourself. Whoever holds the keys, holds the crypto. Ideally keep these keys in cold storage (off-line).

Alternatively, look for custodians that are insured, audited and regulated. Ask what happens to your funds in the event the custodian goes bankrupt? To what extent are your funds insured and by whom? As a best practice, consult an experienced lawyer in the crypto space to help you evaluate any custodial relationship you enter into.

Chapter Four
Hedge Funds

The global hedge fund market is a massive and largely unregulated sector, with over 15,000 hedge funds operating worldwide and approximately $4.5 trillion in combined assets under management as of mid-2022. Of these, roughly two-thirds are based in the United

States and are subject to regulation by the Securities and Exchange Commission (SEC).

In addition to SEC-regulated hedge funds, there are also many offshore hedge funds, which are often located in tax-friendly jurisdictions such as the Cayman Islands or Bermuda. These funds are not subject to the same level of regulatory oversight as their US-based counterparts, which can present both opportunities and risks for investors.

Hedge funds are pooled investments that use a variety of strategies to generate outsized profits for their investors. Unlike traditional mutual funds or exchange-traded funds, hedge funds have few restrictions on their investment choices, giving the hedge fund manager more flexibility to buy and sell a range of assets. These can include stocks, bonds, real estate, derivatives, commodities, and currencies, among other choices. A fund can be long-only or short-only or use a combination of long and short strategies.

While hedge funds often charge higher fees than traditional investment vehicles, the justification for these fees is that they can deliver robust returns for investors, even in down markets. The managers of the largest funds can earn millions of dollars per year, and in some cases, even billions. This is based on fund managers receiving both an incentive fee, which is a percent of the profits they generate (usually between 15-30%), and a management or asset fee, which is a percentage paid to the manager of the total assets they manage (usually between 1-3%).

Overall, the global hedge fund market is a significant and dynamic sector, with a wide range of investment strategies and potential rewards.

Investors should carefully consider the risks and fees associated with hedge funds before deciding to invest, as well as researching the track record and reputation of the fund manager. Additionally, investors should be aware of the regulatory status and location of the fund, as this can have implications for both risk and taxation.

If you are presented with the hedge fund investment opportunity, start by doing some research and what lawyers term, due diligence, into the principals running the hedge fund. Start with this because theoretically, anyone can say they manage a hedge fund.

One notable example of someone who defrauded others by claiming to run a hedge fund is Bernard Madoff. Madoff founded Bernard L. Madoff Investment Securities LLC and claimed to run a highly successful hedge fund. However, in reality, Madoff was running a massive Ponzi scheme, using new investments to pay off earlier investors and falsifying account statements to cover up the fraud. When the scheme finally collapsed in 2008, investors lost billions of dollars.

Another example is the case of Boaz Manor and his associate, Edith Pardo. They claimed to be running a hedge fund called the Canadian Foresight Group, which was purportedly investing in technology startups. However, in reality, the fund was a front for a pump-and-dump scheme, in which Manor and Pardo artificially inflated the stock prices of companies they owned or controlled, then sold their shares for a profit. Manor and Pardo were eventually caught and faced charges of fraud and market manipulation.

In another case, Phillip Boakes, a former Barclays trader, was sentenced to four and a half years in prison for defrauding investors by claiming to run a successful hedge fund. Boakes convinced investors to put money into his fund, promising returns of up to 15% per year. However Boakes was using the money to fund his lavish lifestyle and make payments to earlier investors. When the scheme finally unraveled, investors lost over £3.5 million.

In 2018, Lawrence E. Penn III was charged with defrauding investors out of over $20 million by falsely claiming to be running a hedge fund called Camelot Acquisitions Secondary Opportunity Management. Penn claimed that his hedge fund held assets of over $800 million and that he had a long history of success as a hedge fund manager. The fund had no assets. Penn had no experience or credentials in the industry.

These are just a few examples of individuals who defrauded others by claiming to run successful hedge funds. Investors should always be cautious and thoroughly research any investment opportunity before putting their money at risk.

One of the hallmarks we have observed of fraudsters who pretend to run hedge funds are a lack of appropriate legal documentation such as subscription documents, risk disclosure documents and investment management agreements. Have an attorney review all these documents for you and advise you of what you are signing.

Also look at the brokerage statements and where they come from. We have seen con men fabricate brokerage statements-Bernie Madoff did this. It is worth consulting a lawyer, if at all possible. My law office does a deep dive into due diligence which includes all of the above and much more.

Chapter Five
Registration- What it Means and Why it Matters

As a potential investor, there are numerous benefits to dealing with a registered individual and entity. Registration provides a level of assurance that the party has met specific regulatory requirements and standards, which can help mitigate, though not altogether eliminate, the risk of fraud or other illegal activities. Most frauds and scams occur between investors and unregistered parties, so while registration is no guarantee against fraud, your chances of being a victim of fraud are less and if you were dealing with an unregistered party/entity. This is largely because registered parties are subject to oversight by regulatory bodies, which can help ensure that they are adhering to applicable laws and regulations and they have been vetted by a federal or state agency.

Registered parties are required to disclose certain information to investors, such as financial statements, investment strategies, and other relevant details. This transparency can help investors make informed decisions about whether or not to invest with the party, as well as monitor the performance of their investments.

Furthermore, if an investor experiences any issues or disputes with a registered party, they likely have legal remedies and protections. They are places to go to seek reparations, to file grievances, to be entitled to arbitration of disputes and pursue legal action.

What registration also means, is that a federal or state agency has already done some of the due diligence on a person for you. Being registered with the CFTC usually means the following:

- Registered Principals and associated persons in the derivatives world and the counterparts (Principals and registered representatives) in the securities world, have been fingerprinted and been subjected to background checks.

- The firm has met financial requirements in terms of minimum capitalization, and in some cases is required to meet these requirements on an ongoing basis.

- The location of a registrant's primary place of business and branch offices are verified and accessible to customers.

- Registrants must submit to examinations and regulatory supervision.

- Associated persons and registered representatives have passed licensing exam and meet standards of proficiency requirements.

- Registrants are required to make disclosures at regular intervals and conduct themselves according to set standards.

- Registrants in the futures world are subject to random audits by the NFA.

In the United States, investment advisors are required to register with the Securities and Exchange Commission (SEC) or the appropriate state securities regulator. By doing so, they are subject to disclosure requirements and must adhere to a fiduciary duty to act in their clients' best interests. This provides investors with some assurance that the investment advisor is operating within a regulated framework and is accountable for their actions.

Similarly, broker-dealers must register with FINRA (Financial Industry Regulatory Authority) and are subject to a range of regulatory requirements, including rules regarding fair dealing, disclosure, and supervision. This can help investors to feel more comfortable that the broker-dealer is operating in a transparent and ethical manner.

Overall, investing with a registered party can provide investors with greater transparency, legal protections, and regulatory oversight, which can help mitigate risk and improve their overall investment experience.

There are firms and individuals who may be exempt from registration or not regulated by the CFTC, and they may appear in the NFA BASIC database (referenced below), with a notice of the basis for their exemption. For examples, many Commodity Trading Advisors (CTAs) and Commodity Trading Pools (CPOs), operate under exemptions from full registration, but still have regulatory reporting and compliance obligations.

In case you can't find a firm or person in the NFA BASIC database, it's important to ask them why. Additionally, depending on the product or service offered, it may be necessary to check with other regulatory agencies, which we will cover briefly.

The U.S. has a number of agencies which permit an investor to check their broker, brokerage firm or other financial profession to ensure that they have the proper registration and licensing to offer investments.

To find out if a person claiming to run a hedge fund is registered and that their work experience is what they represent it to be go to: https://brokercheck.finra.org/

FINRA's BrokerCheck will tell you if the person is or was registered, as they are required by law to be to sell securities and/or give investment advice.

Also go to the SEC's website to search for administrative actions taken against an individual: https://www.sec.gov/litigations/sec-action-look-up

The NFA also has a firm and individual database where you can research an individual or firm and see if they are registered, financial information about them, if they have had any disciplinary or administrative actions taken against them and whether their narrative of their past and current professional experience can be verified: https://www.nfa.futures.org/basicnet/

In order to check if an individual or firm is registered as an investment advisor, go the following website: https://adviserinfo.sec.gov/

For insurance products, go here: https://content.naic.org/state-insurance-departments

Other websites to visit to research other investor complaints, enforcement actions and more, include the Consumer Financial Protection Bureau (CFPB), which can be accessed here: https://www.consumerfinance.gov/data-research/consumer-complaints/

Also use Google and the each state's Securities and Exchange Commission counterpart. If at all feasible, call an experienced securities lawyer for help in evaluating a potential hedge fund investment opportunity. Remember that if a hedge fund is located off-shore and it is unregulated, you may have little recourse in the event you are a victim of fraud.

It's important to exercise caution when dealing with unregistered firms or individuals in markets or products that have historically seen numerous incidents of fraud. Such markets include precious metals, binary options, forex, and digital currencies. The futures markets are heavily regulated and as a result, have protections for the safeguarding of customer assets that are among the stringent in the world. Keep in mind that doing business with entities not registered with the CFTC, or even the SEC, exposes you to greater risk, and offers less protection in case of fraud.

Chapter Six
Registration of Digital Currencies (Crypto)

The CFTC regulates products that utilize virtual currencies as their underlying commodity. What this means is that if a financial instrument's value is derived from a virtual currency, such as Bitcoin or Ethereum, it is likely regulated by the CFTC (the authors hedge here because Bitcoin is under the jurisdiction of the CFTC but Ethereum maybe subject to a jurisdictional battle between the SEC and CFTC). For example, a futures contract that allows the buyer to purchase a certain amount of Bitcoin at a future date at a specified price is a product that uses virtual currency as its underlying commodity-it is derived from the currency. Other examples include options contracts and exchange-traded funds (ETFs) that track the price of virtual currencies.

Intermediaries that facilitate trading in these instruments or provide advice to clients regarding virtual currency commodity futures must be registered with both the CFTC and NFA.

Websites or companies that enable customers to buy or trade virtual currencies on the cash or spot market are not required to be registered with the CFTC. However, the CFTC retains general anti-fraud and manipulation enforcement authority over virtual currency cash markets.

Digital currency spot market trading firms and cryptocurrency exchanges like Coinbase, Kraken and Binance.US are classified as money service businesses (MSB) by the U.S. Treasury and must be registered with FinCEN. Many states also mandate that virtual currency trading websites register as money transfer companies. PayPal and Western Union are considered money transmitter businesses.

One caveat about the registration of crypto exchanges as MSBs is that they are not held to the far more stringent regulatory and compliance requirements of regulated CFTC and SEC exchanges. Money transmitters lack the safeguards of CFTC and SEC regulated brokerage firms. Money centers take custody of client assets but they lack the powerful regulatory protections of customer segregated funds that futures commission merchants (FCMs) have under the CFTC. They are not necessarily adequately capitalized or independently audited, and otherwise generally lack the regulatory safeguards of traditionally regulated brokerage firms.

To see if the digital currency trading company you intend to use is registered with FinCEN, check the MSB Registrant Search: https://www.fincen.gov/msb-registrant-search

Also, check the Nationwide Multistate Licensing System (NMLS) to see if the company is registered in your state, which is managed by the Conference of State Bank Supervisors. You can do this by going here: https://www.csbs.org/nationwide-multistate-licensing-system

Registration with FinCEN and the NMLS indicates that:

- The firm adheres to federal anti-money laundering laws.
- The location of the firm's headquarters.
- The company is bound by federal and state laws.

If necessary, you may also be able to file complaints with your state banking regulator. Remember that you may have no protections if you choose an unregistered, offshore firm.

Chapter Seven

Partnership Investments

A limited partnership is a type of partnership where there are two types of partners: general partners and limited partners. The general partner is responsible for managing the partnership and making decisions, while the limited partner's liability is limited to the amount of their investment. If you are presented with an opportunity to invest in a business or venture structured as a partnership, the odds are you are being invited to become a limited partner.

The main advantage of a limited partnership interest is that you are shielded from personal liability. Limited partners are not personally liable for the partnership's debts and obligations beyond their initial investment. There are also tax benefits and other advantages but this guide's purpose is to provide the downsides and not to cheerlead any particular investment. There are many downsides to investing in a limited partnership which you should be aware of.

One disadvantage of investing in a limited partnership is that the limited partner has little control over the partnership's operations. The general partner is responsible for making all decisions, and the limited partner has no say in how the partnership is run. This lack of control can be a significant disadvantage for investors who want to have a say in how their money is invested. This also means you have to trust in the business acumen and integrity of the general partners.

Another disadvantage of investing in a limited partnership is that while the limited partner's liability is limited only to the amount of their investment and the limited partner's personal assets are not at risk, if the partnership incurs debt or is sued, and incurs more debt than it can pay, the limited partner could lose their entire investment.

Perhaps the main downside of limited partnerships is that they are illiquid investments. It can be difficult to sell the investment and get your money back. Unlike publicly traded stocks or mutual funds, which can be bought and sold daily, limited partnership interests are typically sold through private transactions, which can be time-consuming and may not generate the desired return. There is generally no aftermarket for limited partnership interests. And even if you found a potential buyer for your limited partnership stake, the partnership agreement may prohibit you from transferring or selling your interest or place restrictive covenants on your ability to do so.

Another disadvantage of investing in a limited partnership is that they often have high fees. General partners typically charge management fees and may also take a share of the profits, which can reduce the limited partner's return on investment.

Limited partnerships often invest in assets such as real estate or private equity, which are not without risk.

An analogous investment to a limited partnership is a private equity investment. Like limited partnerships, private equity investments involve investing in private companies or assets that are not publicly traded on an exchange. Private equity investments are often structured as limited partnerships, with investors serving as limited partners and the private equity firm serving as the general partner.

While limited partnerships can provide investors with the opportunity to invest in arguably higher risk, higher-return assets, they also come with a range of disadvantages, including lack of control, illiquidity, high fees, and higher risk. It is important to consider each of these factors before investing. Ideally, it makes sense to consult a financial advisor for guidance on whether an investment like this suits your risk tolerance profile and investment time horizon.

It is crucial to understand the partnership agreement and all subscription documents, including all risk disclosure statements. Sometimes, they may contain lock-up clauses which prevent you from liquidating your interests for a specific period of time, or other restrictions on sale or transfer.

Chapter Eight
AI, ESG and the Next Big Thing

AI holds tremendous promise for the future and is already changing the face of business and the law. The transformational potential of generative AI is only now being beginning to be understood. Unfortunately, as with any emerging and rapidly evolving industry, there is always a risk of fraudulent activity. And because so little is known by the investment class and financial and legal professionals about the process of creating AI systems, this area has seen and will see many fraudulent investment schemes that are difficult for most people to discern as such.

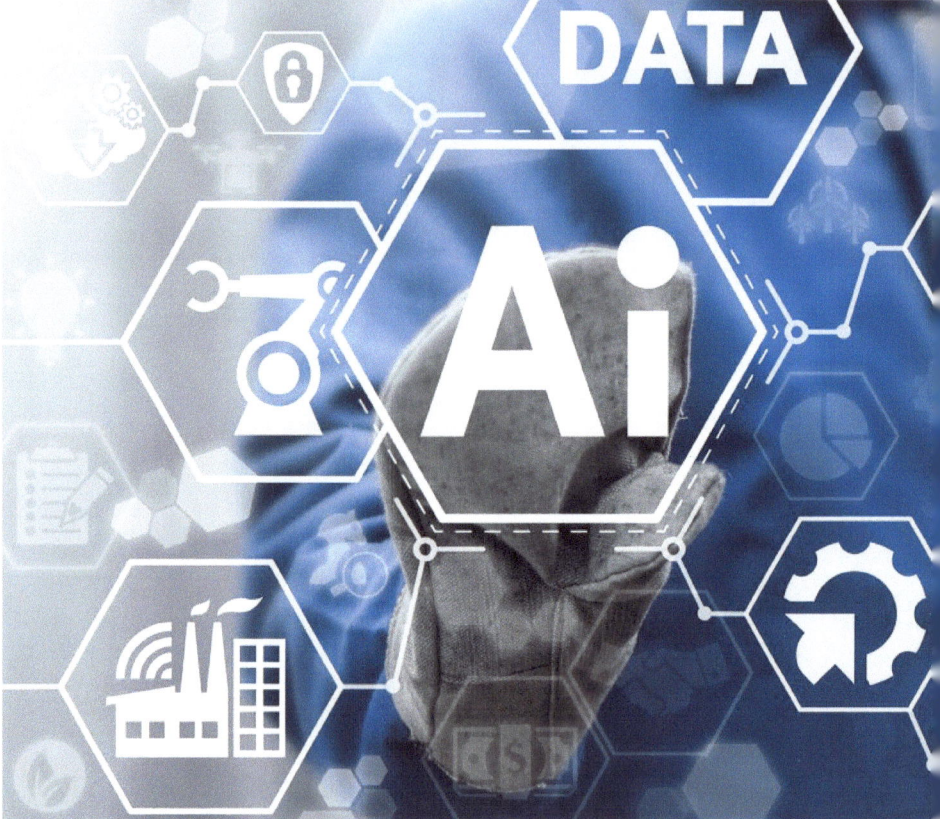

Some of the most common types of AI investment scams we have already observed include:

Fake AI investment funds: Fraudsters may claim to manage an AI investment fund that generates high returns by using advanced algorithms and machine learning. In reality, the fund may not exist or may not use any AI technology.

One example of a fraudulent AI investment scheme and fake AI product is seen in the case of Anna Sorokin, also known as Anna Delvey. Anna Delvey, who is the subject of the Netflix series Inventing Anna, was sentenced to prison in 2019 for multiple charges including grand larceny and theft of services. Ms. Sorokin posed as a wealthy German heiress and convinced investors to fund her luxury lifestyle and a supposed art foundation. Ms. Sorokin claimed her foundation would use AI to curate exhibitions. However, the foundation turned out to be a complete fabrication, and Sorokin used all the funds for personal expenses.

Fake AI products or services: Fraudsters may promote AI products or services that do not actually exist or do not work as advertised. These scams may involve selling fake AI software or offering AI-powered investment advice.

Pump and dump schemes: Fraudsters may artificially inflate the price of an AI stock by spreading false or misleading information about the company's technology or financial performance. Once the stock price has increased, the fraudsters sell their shares for a profit, leaving other investors with worthless shares.

Ponzi schemes: Fraudsters may use AI-related jargon to attract investors to a Ponzi scheme, where they use new investor funds to pay earlier investors. These schemes eventually collapse when there are not enough new investors to sustain the payouts.

An example of this is the case of the "AI-powered" cryptocurrency investment scheme called GAW Miners, which turned out to be a Ponzi scheme. The company claimed to use AI algorithms to mine cryptocurrencies and offered investors guaranteed returns. Unfortunately, GAW Miners was fraudulent scheme that misused investor funds and eventually collapsed.

Investors should be cautious of any investment opportunity related to AI and conduct thorough research before investing. It is important to seek expert advice to verify the legitimacy of the investment opportunity. It is only by establishing the legitimacy of the alleged investment opportunity that the risks involved can be understood.

Here a word of advice-just because someone is extremely well qualified on paper, does not mean the AI investment is automatically sound. There will be fits and starts as AI develops and there are many participants working in this field-not all of whom will succeed. Look beyond the credentials of the AI team to evaluate the investment itself because ultimately, this is what you are investing in. This is why, seeking expert help is highly advisable no matter how compelling the investment pitch.

Like the field of AI, ESG (Environmental, Social and Governance) investments are having their moment. And like any investment opportunity, ESG investments are not immune to fraud. Here again, be aware of people who are just trying to ride the wave of the next big thing and seek expert advice.

There have already been examples of ESG investment fraud. ESG investing has become increasingly popular in recent years as investors seek to align their investments with their values and beliefs.

One example of ESG investment fraud is the case of the Woodbridge Group of Companies, which was charged by the US Securities and Exchange Commission (SEC) in 2017 for operating a Ponzi scheme. The Woodbridge Group claimed to be investing in real estate projects that were environmentally and socially responsible, but, the company was using new investor money to pay off earlier investors. The company raised over $1.2 billion from investors and filed for bankruptcy in 2017.

Another example is the case of the Sustainvest Asset Management, LLC, which was charged by the SEC in 2019 for making false statements about its investment strategy. The company claimed to use a socially responsible investment strategy, but, the company did not have any ESG criteria and was investing in companies that did not meet its advertised ESG standards.

The SEC and CFTC have yet to issue a regulatory regime for ESG investments or guidance beyond the prohibition of greenwashing. Greenwashing is a marketing tactic used by companies to make their products or services appear more environmentally friendly than they actually are. This can include making false or exaggerated claims about the environmental benefits of their products or services or creating a misleading impression through the use of green imagery, colors, or slogans.

The term "greenwashing" was coined in the 1980s by environmental activist Jay Westerveld, who used the term to describe hotels that encouraged guests to reuse towels for environmental reasons but did not take any other significant steps to reduce their environmental impact.

Examples of greenwashing include companies claiming their products are "100% natural" or "organic" when they are not, or using vague or unregulated terms such as "sustainable" or "eco-friendly" without providing specific details to back up their claims. Greenwashing can also occur when companies use green imagery or slogans to create a misleading impression of environmental friendliness, without actually making any substantive changes to their practices.

One of the issues facing investors and advisor looking at ESG investments is the lack of a global taxonomy or system of globally agreed upon metrics and standards for compliance or measurement. This problem will continue to plague ESG investments for some time, and it is unfortunate. Another issue facing advisors and investors looking critically at ESG investment products and decks is the inherent amorphousness of the terms "social" and "governance." What this means is it is all the more important to make sure the investment and its executive team are sound.

Greenwashing is problematic because it can mislead consumers into making choices that are not actually environmentally beneficial, and can also undermine legitimate efforts to promote sustainability and reduce environmental impact. To avoid greenwashing, consumers can research products and companies before making purchases, look for independent certifications or third-party verification of environmental claims, and be wary of vague or unsubstantiated claims of environmental friendliness.

My law practice has seen a surge of investment decks with various ESG claims, some to garner favorable tax credits or attract investment from asset managers with ESG targets. Suffice it to say, not all ESG investment opportunities, like any other type of investment, are created equal. It is important to research the investment products and the companies they are investing in, and look for independent verification of ESG claims. It is also important to understand the risks associated with any investment opportunity, including the risk of fraud as this is a "hot" area of investment, and like AI, legitimately, one of the next big things.

If at all possible, consult an expert in AI or machine learning when evaluating an AI investment. Find an expert, or failing that, a lawyer versed in the field of regulatory matters to help conduct due diligence on an ESG idea. Also remember to use the resources for checking out the principles of an investment enumerated in Chapters

Six and Seven.

Chapter Nine
Red Flags

All that glisters is not gold--
Often have you heard that told.
Many a man his life hath sold
But my outside to behold.
Gilded tombs do worms infold.
Had you been as wise as bold,
Young in limbs, in judgment old...
      William Shakespeare, Merchant of Venice

Be aware of common red flags:

- Guaranteed returns: If an investment is offering guaranteed returns, especially if they are higher than what is typically available in the market. No investment is completely risk-free, and higher returns typically come with higher risk. Nothing is guaranteed other than death and taxes.

- Pressure to act quickly: Fraudsters often use high-pressure tactics to get potential investors to act quickly, such as claiming that the investment opportunity is only available for a limited time. Legitimate investment opportunities allow investors time to carefully consider the investment and make an informed decision.

- Lack of transparency: If the investment opportunity does not provide clear and transparent information about the investment, such as how it works, where the money is going, and who is managing the investment, it is a major red flag.

- Unregistered investments: Many legitimate investments are required to be registered with regulatory authorities such as the SEC or FINRA. If the investment opportunity is not registered, it could be a sign of a fraudulent investment.

- Unsolicited offers: Be wary of unsolicited offers, especially those that come via cold calls, emails, or social media messages. Especially emails and social media.

- Promises of insider information: Fraudsters may claim to have insider information about a particular company or industry that they can use to generate profits. However, using insider information for trading is illegal, and such promises are often a sign of a fraudulent investment.

- It seems too good to be true...it probably is not true.

- A rare opportunity to own precious metals, gold bullion bars...from the mine or source-

Bullion coin scams: In a bullion coin scam, fraudsters may try to sell investors coins made from rare metals such as gold or silver at inflated prices. The coins may be marketed as a rare or unique investment opportunity, but in reality, they may be overpriced or even fake.

Mining scams: In a mining scam, fraudsters may claim to have discovered a valuable deposit of rare metals and may offer investors the opportunity to invest in the mining operation. These scams may involve promises of high returns, but in reality, the mining operation may not exist, or the deposit may not be as valuable as advertised.

Exploration scams: In an exploration scam, fraudsters may claim to be conducting exploration activities for rare metals and may offer investors the opportunity to invest in the exploration effort. These scams may involve promises of high returns, but in reality, the exploration activities may not be real or may not be as valuable as advertised.

Storage scams: In a storage scam, fraudsters may offer investors the opportunity to store rare metals in a secure facility. These scams may involve promises of high returns or low storage fees, but in reality, the storage facility may not exist, or the metals may not be as valuable as advertised.

- A microcap stock (penny stock) play that only you are being told about...beware of a marketplace that can be illiquid and subject to manipulation

- Get rich FX (Forex market) trading scheme-

  <u>Fake trading platforms:</u> Some fraudulent companies may create fake online trading platforms that appear to be legitimate FX trading platforms. These platforms may have charts, graphs, and other features that give the appearance of a professional trading environment. However, these platforms are often rigged to ensure that investors lose money, and the fraudulent companies may use various tactics to prevent investors from withdrawing their funds.

  <u>Guaranteed profits</u>: Fraudulent companies may offer guaranteed profits to investors, often using high-pressure sales tactics to get them to invest. These profits may be advertised as being generated through legitimate FX trading

activities, but in reality, they are often a result of the fraudulent scheme.

Misrepresentation of trading activities: Some fraudulent companies may misrepresent their trading activities, making it seem like they are conducting legitimate FX trading activities. They may claim to have access to exclusive trading strategies, inside information, or other advantages that enable them to generate high profits. However, these claims are often false, and the companies may not actually be engaged in any real trading activities.

Pyramid schemes: Some fraudulent companies may operate as pyramid schemes, using new investor funds to pay off older investors. These schemes rely on a constant stream of new investors to keep the scheme going, and they often collapse when new investor funds dry up.

Chapter Ten
Single Points of Failure

There is a single point of failure in the context of investments that we have seen time and time again in regards to professional athletes, medical professionals and many others who trust the reward for their life's worth to a single law firm, agent or financial advisor. This is akin to putting all your eggs into one basket. It refers to a situation where the failure of one financial advisor or investment can cause significant losses for an investor. A single point of failure is especially harmful to professional athletes who have a relatively amount of time in which they make most of the money they will ever earn playing professional sports.

For example, when a professional athlete relies on a single financial advisor for all their investment decisions, and that advisor makes a mistake or engages in fraudulent activities, that athlete can lose everything they have worked so gain over a lifetime.

Former NBA star Scottie Pippen has spoken publicly about a single point of failure in his financial management. In 2005, the former Chicago Bulls star, initiated a lawsuit for legal malpractice against the law firm that convinced him to hire a financial advisor who lost millions of dollars through questionable investments. The lawsuit claims that Katten Muchen Zavis Rosenman and one of its attorneys, Sheldon T. Zenner, were negligent and had a conflict of interest when they recommended Robert Lunn, a client of Katten Muchen, as a financial advisor. Lunn had worked at two investment banks and was well regarded as a power broker and friend of Chicago's elite. Interestingly enough Lunn had managed to lie about attending University of Chicago but this was never discovered.

After several years, Scottie Pippen realized that Lunn had forged his name to take out loans, which Lunn then used to pay of his own personal debts. Robert Lunn was ultimately convicted of fraud and served a three-year sentence.

But Pippen's case is not unique among professional athletes. Yes, there have been many cases of professional athletes who have been defrauded by their financial advisors. Athletes, particularly those who earn significant sums of money during their careers, are often targeted by unscrupulous advisors who take advantage of their trust and lack of financial knowledge.

One example is former NFL player Terrell Owens, who in 2019 sued his former financial advisor, claiming that the advisor had mismanaged his investments and caused him to lose millions of dollars. Owens alleged that his advisor had made risky investments without his knowledge or consent and had charged excessive fees for his services.

Another example is former NBA player Latrell Sprewell, who in 2011 filed for bankruptcy after losing most of his earnings to bad investments and financial mismanagement. Sprewell had reportedly trusted his financial advisor to make investment decisions on his behalf, but the advisor had made a series of poor investments that resulted in significant losses.

Former NFL quarterback Mark Sanchez also filed a lawsuit against his former financial advisor in 2019, alleging that the advisor had steered him into risky and fraudulent investments that caused him to lose millions of dollars. Sanchez alleged that his advisor had engaged in a Ponzi scheme and had misled him about the true nature of the investments.

These are just a few examples of the many cases of professional athletes who have been defrauded by their financial advisors. It highlights the importance of athletes, other high net worth individuals, and everyone else, being careful when selecting their financial advisors and taking steps to protect themselves against financial fraud.

Regardless of how connected or well-placed your financial advisor is, we recommend that at least once a year, preferably twice, you hire an outside lawyer to conduct a spot audit of your finances. This can be as simple as giving the attorney the authority to request statements, at random, directly from your bank and brokerage accounts. As well as monitoring the fees charged by an advisor and the current financial status of any financial ventures or investments. Few law firms offer this service, we do and it is important. If for some unfortunate reason, you cannot hire a securities lawyer to perform this type of audit, be sure you request and look at the statements (generated directly from your brokerage houses and bank(s)) at least once, if not twice a year, yourself.

In closing, with this guide, we hope you will borrow the jaundiced eyesight of two well-meaning securities and derivatives lawyers, who do not want to see you become the victim of financial fraud. While this guide is not legal advice and is certainly no substitute for the value of such advice, we hope it has given you some things to think about in viewing an investment, and some tools to do your own research everyone who you trust with you money.

Be as risk averse and skeptical as a bank that will only give you an umbrella when the sun is out, or a loan when you are so flush with cash and have a credit score so good that you don't need it -and then take it away when it rains. Unfortunately, your odds of investing in the ultimate get rich scheme are higher than the odds of it being either legitimate or successful-unless you adopt a skeptical footing.@

R Tamara de Silva, Esq. & Cheryl Fitzpatrick-Smith, Esq.

Appendix of Resources

To investigate firms/individuals/brokers/financial advisors

Futures markets:

https://www.nfa.futures.org/basicnet/

Securities markets:

https://brokercheck.finra.org/

https://adviserinfo.sec.gov/

Administrative/disciplinary/enforcement actions:

https://www.sec.gov/litigations/sec-action-look-up

https://www.cftc.gov/LearnAndProtect/Resources/Check/redlist.htm

https://www.sec.gov/enforce/public-alerts

https://www.consumerfinance.gov/data-research/consumer-complaints/

Digital assets/crypto registration:

https://www.fincen.gov/msb-registrant-search

https://www.csbs.org/nationwide-multistate-licensing-system

Insurance:

https://content.naic.org/state-insurance-departments

Bank deposits:

https://banks.data.fdic.gov/bankfind-suite/

There are hundreds of parties that impersonate registered parties, or claim to be registered and are not -and are operating crypto firms and funds, be sure to also cross check this list:

https://www.sec.gov/enforce/public-alerts

To investigate firms/individuals/brokers/financial advisors in the UK

https://www.fca.org.uk/firms/financial-services-register

https://register.fca.org.uk/s/

Research European Union entities/individuals

https://www.esma.europa.eu/investor-corner

https://www.iosco.org/investor_protection/?subsection=investor_alerts_portal

Canada

https://info.securities-administrators.ca/nrsmobile/nrssearch.aspx

Cheryl Fitzpatrick is Deputy Chief Compliance Officer of ADM. She is also the Founder of Futures Compliance, Inc.

Cheryl has decades of experience advising brokerages, brokers, hedge funds, trading groups and other futures industry registrants and participants on registration and compliance matters in the derivatives industry.

She has trained personnel, created compliance procedures, performed audits, defended audits; arbitrations; litigation; mediation; drafting, negotiation and review of industry agreements; crisis consulting and risk mitigation.

R Tamara de Silva is a securities lawyer who founded a law firm specializing in comprehensive securities investment consulting and audit services in various investment advisory products and services, including investment fund products, separately managed accounts, structured products, and all kinds of funds, including investments in digital assets and ESG.

Tamara examines investment decks, deals, and agreements on behalf of family offices, asset managers, and high net worth investors. Her analysis entails conducting extensive due diligence, in-depth analysis, as well as spot audits of third-party investment advisor relationships. Tamara has worked as a derivatives and securities lawyer for 24 years with a securities practice involving regulation and compliance as well as white collar criminal defense.

www.ingramcontent.com/pod-product-compliance
Lightning Source LLC
Chambersburg PA
CBHW041146210326
41519CB00046B/156